Joseph Smith
Teenage Prophet

RICHARD E. TURLEY JR.

Produced by
Church History and Doctrine
Publishing

Available at Amazon.com

ISBN: 9781652956396

1 3 5 7 9 10 8 6 4 2

Cover image: Detail from the first visual
depiction of Joseph Smith's First Vision
published as frontispiece to chapter one of
T. B. H. Stenhouse's *The Rocky Mountain
Saints* (New York: D. Appleton, 1873)

Ask, and it shall be given you;
seek, and ye shall find.
—Matthew 7:7

CONTENTS

1 BIRTH

"I was born in the town of Sharon in the state of Vermont, North America, on the twenty-third day of December A.D. 1805 of goodly parents who spared no pains to instructing me in the Christian religion."[1] That is how Joseph Smith Jr. began a personal history he wrote by hand, likely in the summer of 1832 when he was twenty-six years old. These opening lines tell a lot about his birth and upbringing.

The United States, where he entered the world, was a young nation at the time. Thomas Jefferson was the nation's president, only the third in the country's history. The year before Joseph's birth, Mr. Jefferson sent out Meriwether Lewis and William Clark on their famed expedition to explore the Louisiana Purchase. The members of their Corps of Discovery had reached the Pacific Ocean and constructed Fort Clatsop, near the mouth of the Columbia River, where they were spending the winter on Joseph's birthdate.[2]

Although Joseph Smith later became famous in New York state, he spent his first decade as a New Englander. His birthplace in Vermont was a bit more than eighty miles south of the U.S.-Canada border, as the crow flies, and Joseph chose to write that he was born in North America, not the United States—evidence, perhaps, that he interacted with both Americans and Canadians in his early years.[3]

The America of Joseph's birth was not the United States of today. Geographically, it was much smaller. Politically, it was different too. Though the Declaration of Independence proclaimed "that all men are created equal," the America of Joseph's day was divided into classes, depending on circumstances, one of which was property ownership.[4] His parents, Joseph Smith Sr. and Lucy Mack Smith, were originally among the landed class. But then Joseph's father found himself swindled in a business venture, and they had to sell their property to cover debts.[5]

As a result, when Joseph Jr. was born, his parents were renting Lucy's father's farm, and over the next decade they moved from place to place, struggling to make a living as tenant farmers.[6]

2 SICKNESS

Meanwhile, sickness struck the Smith family as a typhoid fever epidemic swept through the region of New England where they were living.[7] This infectious bacterial disease struck down all the Smith children, including Joseph. "At one time, during my sickness, my father despaired of my life," Joseph recalled. "The doctors broke the fever, after which it settled under my shoulder. . . . Dr. Parker called it a sprained shoulder and anointed it with bone ointment, and freely applied the hot shovel, when it proved to be a swelling under the arm, which was opened and discharged freely, after which the disease removed and descended into my left leg and ankle and terminated in a fever sore of the worst kind."[8]

Joseph's lower leg swelled horribly with the infection. Doctors slit the leg open down to the bone between knee and ankle to relieve the pressure and pain, and they talked of amputation. After some discussion, they instead applied a pioneering medical technique that was well ahead of its time for curing the disease. Again slicing the leg open, they drilled holes in Joseph's leg bone— one below the knee, the other above the ankle— and used forceps to snap off pieces of the bone between the holes.[9]

Lucy Mack Smith, Joseph's mother, had left the room and moved about a hundred yards away to avoid hearing her boy's agonizing cries during the surgery. She left this account:

> The surgeons began by boring into the bone—first on one side of the affected part, then on the other—after which they broke it loose with a pair of forceps or pincers. Thus, they took away two large pieces of the bone. When they broke off the first piece, he [Joseph] screamed so loud . . . that I could not repress my desire of going to him. But as soon as I entered the room, he cried out, "Oh, Mother! Go back! Go back! I do not want you to come in. I will tough it if you will go."

When the third fracture was . . . taken away, I burst into the room again and oh! . . . what a spectacle for a mother's eye: the wound torn open to view, my boy and the bed on which he [lay] covered with . . . blood which . . . was still gushing from the wound. He was pale as a corpse and . . . big drops of sweat were rolling down his face, every feature of which depicted agony that cannot be described.

I was forced from the room and detained till they finished the operation.[10]

Imagine suffering such trauma as Joseph did at age seven. The surgery was gruesome, but it ultimately proved successful. He "now began to recover," Lucy said, "and when . . . he was able to travel . . . he went with his uncle Jesse Smith to Salem [Massachusetts] for the benefit of his health, hoping that the sea breezes might help him. In this we were not disappointed, for he soon became strong and healthy."[11]

When Lucy said Joseph "became strong and healthy," she spoke in relative terms. Joseph suffered from the effects of the surgery for the rest of his life.[12] Besides the nine large pieces of bone that doctors removed from his leg during the surgery, others later worked their way to the surface.[13] "Fourteen additional pieces of bone afterwards worked out before my leg healed," Joseph remembered, "during which time I was reduced so very low that my mother could carry me with ease. And after I began to get about, I went on crutches till I started for the state of New York."[14]

Other sources suggest that Joseph suffered from a slight limp for the rest of his life and was deemed unfit for the military service required at that time for nearly all American males between the ages of fourteen and forty-five.[15]

3 BULLIED

Being unable to walk without crutches for years—and having to hobble or limp after that—restricted Joseph's youthful physical activities and also made him vulnerable to bullying. When his family moved to New York after years of crop failures in New England, his father went ahead of Lucy and the children to find opportunity and a place for them to live. Lucy, in the meantime, sold most of their meager possessions to move herself and the children to their new destination, Palmyra village along the Erie Canal.[16]

Joseph left this account of what happened to him as they moved west:

> I went on crutches till I started for the state of New York, where in the meantime my father had gone . . . for the purpose of

preparing a place for the removal of his family, which he affected by sending a man after . . . us by the name of Caleb Howard. . . . We fell in with a family by the name of Gates who were travelling west, and Howard drove me from the wagon and made me travel in my weak state through the snow forty miles per day for several days, during which time I suffered the most excruciating weariness and pain. And all this that Mr. Howard might enjoy the society of two of Mr. Gates's daughters, which he took on the wagon where I should have rode.

And thus he continued to do day . . . after day through the journey. And when my brothers remonstrated with Mr. Howard for his treatment to me, he would knock them down with the butt of his whip.

. . . On our way from Utica, I was left to ride on the last wagon [or] sleigh in the company. (The Gates family were in sleighs.) But when that came up, I was knocked down by the driver, one of Gates's sons, and left to wallow in my blood until a stranger came along, picked me up, and carried me to the town of Palmyra.[17]

And that is how young Joseph Smith Jr., then just ten or eleven years old, made it to Palmyra, New York, in late 1816 or early 1817.

4 AWAKENING

When Joseph and his family reached Palmyra, the village was in the midst of a period of spiritual revival. James Harvey Hotchkin, an ordained Protestant minister and historian of the period, put it this way:

> In September 1816, it was stated that, in Palmyra, a glorious work had commenced, that many were rejoicing in hope, while multitudes were inquiring the way of salvation. About 120 hopeful converts are stated on the minutes of the Synod, as the result of this effusion of the Holy Spirit. Geneva [near Palmyra] is also mentioned as a place where there was an increased attention to the things of religion, and some hopeful subjects of divine grace. In Middlesex (now Rushville) there was a revival

of great power and extent, as the result of which, 100 or more united with the church, and, according to the testimony of the present pastor, nearly all remained steadfast in the faith. At the same time, Gorham (now Hopewell), was visited with the showers of the Spirit, and a goodly number were hopefully converted to God.[18]

In an age when religious revivals attracted a great deal of attention from townsfolk, it is no surprise that young Joseph Smith Jr. noticed them.

Camp meetings or revivals, along with elections and militia musters, were among the biggest events of the year in many communities.[19] For poor children like those in the Smith family, school did not occupy a lot of time. In Joseph's 1832 history, he wrote:

> My father, Joseph Smith Sr., [and my mother] . . . being in indigent circumstances were obliged to labor hard for the support of a large family, having nine children. And as it required [the] exertions of all that were able to render any assistance for the support of the family, therefore we were deprived of the benefit of an education. Suffice it to say I was merely instructed in reading and writing and

the ground rules of arithmetic, which constituted my whole literary acquirements.[20]

Though Joseph had, as he said, little formal education, he did know how to read, and given his physical handicap, you might expect he would use books as an escape from the cares of the world. But that wasn't the case. Lucy Mack Smith, his mother, explained, "Joseph was less inclined to the study of books than any child we had but much more given to reflection and deep study."[21]

Take a young man who is given to pondering and put him in the middle of an area excited by religious revival, and it is not surprising that he might begin to think deeply about the topic. In his 1832 history, Joseph recorded:

At about the age of twelve years, my mind become seriously impressed with regard to the all-important concerns of . . . the welfare of my immortal soul, which led me to searching the scriptures, believing, as I was taught, that they contained the word of God. Thus applying myself to them, and my intimate acquaintance with those of different denominations, led me to marvel exceedingly, for I discovered that they did not adorn . . . their profession by a holy walk and godly conversation agreeable to what I found contained in that sacred depository. This was a grief to my soul.[22]

Joseph was not only disturbed by seeing the differences between what people professed and how they lived, but he was also concerned about his own sins and weaknesses. His 1832 history observes:

> Thus, from the age of twelve years to fifteen, I pondered many things in my heart concerning the situation of the world of mankind, the contentions and divisions, the wickedness and abominations and the darkness which pervaded . . . the minds of mankind. My mind become exceedingly distressed, for I become convicted of my sins, . . . and I felt to mourn for my own sins and for the sins of the world.[23]

5 PONDERING

Around January 1819, right in the middle of this period of pondering that Joseph described, his family moved some two miles south of Palmyra village to a hundred-acre farm site that they hoped to purchase, a farm that would at last restore them to the status of landholders and provide food, shelter, cash crops, and security for them.[24]

The hundred acres were largely covered with old-growth New York forest, which meant trees hundreds of years old and several feet in circumference.[25] Using just hand tools and draft animals, Joseph Smith Sr. and his boys had to chop and saw down many acres of trees, plow the wild ground, and plant crops. It was backbreaking work that required long hours outdoors. Using the readily available lumber on the property, the Smiths built a snug log home in which to eat and sleep, though like most farmers in their day, they spent most of their time outdoors working the land.[26]

As most people who love the outdoors know, there is something inspiring about being in the middle of the wilderness, which is where Joseph's family were trying to build their farm. Even today, visitors who walk through the old-growth forest on the Smith farm find inspiration in observing the trees, the undergrowth, and the wildlife there.

Joseph was no different. Living and working outdoors day after day, he had a chance to ponder nature. In his 1832 history, he remembered:

> I looked upon the sun—the glorious luminary of the earth—and also the moon, rolling in their majesty through the heavens, and also the stars shining in their courses, and the earth also upon which I stood, and the beast of the field and the fowls of heaven and the fish of the waters, and also man walking forth upon the face of the earth . . . And when I considered upon these things, my heart exclaimed, "Well hath the wise man said . . . it

is a fool that saith in his heart there is no God." My heart exclaimed, "All . . . these bear testimony and bespeak an omnipotent and omnipresent power, a being . . . who was and is and will be from all eternity to eternity."[27]

In this way—through studying the scriptures, pondering, and praying during his earliest teen years—Joseph gained a personal testimony that God lives.

6 FEELING NOTHING

During this period of pondering that led up to his fifteenth year, Joseph remained interested in the revivals that continued to crisscross the region, ebbing and flowing. One of these waves swept through after the family moved out to the farm. In his later history, Joseph explained:

Sometime in the second year after our removal to [the farm], there was in the place where we lived an unusual excitement on the subject of religion. It commenced with the Methodists but soon became general among all the sects in that region of country. Indeed, the whole district of country seemed affected by it, and great multitudes united themselves to the different religious parties, which created no small stir and division among the people, some crying, "Lo here," and some "Lo there." Some were contending for the Methodist faith, some for the Presbyterian, and some for the Baptist . . . . I was at this time in my fifteenth year. My father's family . . . were proselyted to the Presbyterian faith, and four of them joined that church, namely, my mother Lucy, my brothers Hyrum [and] Samuel Harrison, and my sister Sophronia.[28]

Understanding Joseph's feelings at the time requires seeing all this through his teenage eyes. From Joseph's point of view, the religious revivalism was splitting his family. He described how members of the various religious groups were contending with each other. Now, suddenly, he found his family divided into at least three factions.

Joseph Smith Sr., his father, had long differed from his wife, Lucy Mack Smith, on religious matters. Joseph Sr. came from a line of men who dissented from the state church and found greater solace in personal spirituality than in organized religion.[29] Lucy, on the other hand, longed for the social respectability that came from land ownership and the dignity of well-established church groups like the Presbyterians.[30]

Joseph Jr. found himself drawn toward the Methodists, a fast-growing frontier group that, along with the Baptists, was sweeping through much of America, attracting the earthy people who cared more about personally experiencing the Spirit of God than belonging to establishment churches.[31]

This meant Joseph found himself disagreeing with his parents on religious matters at a critical time. More than anything, he wanted relief from his sins, and he assumed that relief would come through finding and joining the right church. A friend later recorded, "Brother Joseph told us . . . he had a revival meeting. His mother and brother and sister got religion. He wanted to get religion too, wanted to feel and shout like the rest, but could feel nothing."[32]

7 A MENTOR

With Joseph's leanings toward Methodism, how could he talk with his father, who looked down on organized religion, or his mother, who found what she liked among the Presbyterians and wanted him to join her for the sake of increased family unity? Like some teenagers who can't speak to their parents about delicate matters, Joseph felt drawn to an adult leader he greatly respected.

Describing this time of Joseph's life, his friend Oliver Cowdery, who heard the story from him, wrote in 1834:

> One Mr. Lane, a presiding elder of the Methodist church, visited Palmyra and vicinity. Elder Lane was a talented man possessing a good share of literary endowments and

apparent humility. There was a great awakening or excitement raised on the subject of religion, and much enquiry for the word of life. Large additions were made to the Methodist, Presbyterian, and Baptist churches. Mr. Lane's manner of communication was peculiarly calculated to awaken the intellect of the hearer and arouse the sinner to look about him for safety. Much good instruction was always drawn from his discourses on the scriptures, and in common with others, our brother's [Joseph's] mind became awakened.[33]

Why Joseph found George Lane's preaching to be appealing can be gleaned from an account of a revival held in western New York in September 1819. Reverend George Peck wrote of that occasion:

On the 13th of September there was a camp-meeting held near Carpenter's Notch, which I attended. Marmaduke Pierce preached a short but mighty sermon and closed with a perfect storm. He addressed the wicked with tremendous power, and then, exclaiming, "I feel the Spirit of God upon me, glory, hallelujah!" dropped down upon the seat behind him, shouting, weeping, laughing, wonderfully moved. The joyous responses from the preachers and the assemblage arose like the sound of many waters, while the whole congregation shook like the forest in a mighty wind. The exhortations of the presiding elder, George Lane, were overwhelming. Sinners quailed under them, and many cried aloud for mercy. The meeting included the Sabbath and continued about a week. Sixty persons professed to find peace, and thirty joined the church.[34]

Joseph Smith admired George Lane and his exhortations, but he had a hard time getting into the Pentecostal ecstasies of many who attended the camp meetings. What he really wanted to know was how to get a sure witness for himself.

8 DETERMINATION

If Joseph's brother William Smith recollected properly many decades later, one thing that impressed Joseph about George Lane was a sermon in which he explained how someone could get that personal witness. William recalled:

A Rev. Mr. Lane of the Methodists preached a sermon on "what church shall I join?" And the burden of his discourse was to ask God, using as a text, "If any man lack wisdom let him ask of God who giveth to all men liberally." And, of course, when Joseph went home and was looking over the text, he was impressed to do just what the preacher had said.[35]

As Joseph explained later, when he read the verse, he had a powerful spiritual experience, the most powerful of his life to that point. He recorded:

> Never did any passage of scripture come with more power to the heart of man than this did at this time to mine. It seemed to enter with great force into every feeling of my heart. I reflected on it again and again, knowing that if any person needed wisdom from God, I did. For how to act I did not know, and unless I could get more wisdom than I then had, [I] would never know.[36]

"At length," Joseph wrote, "I came to the conclusion that I must either remain in darkness and confusion, or else I must do as James directs, that is, Ask of God. I at last came to the determination to ask of God."[37]

9 PRIVATE PRAYER

Where would a fourteen-year-old Joseph Smith go to find privacy? Not to his own room in the Smith house, because—like most poor boys of his generation—he did not have his own room. The Smith boys slept together in the upper loft of the snug log home.[38] Privacy was not to be found in the small house for the large family but rather out away from it. In his 1832 account, Joseph said he went to pray "in the wilderness"—the old-growth forest near his home.[39]

He had already picked out the spot in his mind, later calling it "the place where I had previously designed to go."[40] He knew the place because he had been out in the forest chopping trees there. In an 1843 interview, Joseph described what happened next as follows:

I immediately went out into the woods where my father had a clearing, and went to the stump where I had stuck my axe when I had quit work, and I kneeled down, and prayed, saying, "O Lord, what church shall I join?" Directly I saw a light, and then a glorious personage in the light, and then another personage. And the first personage said to the second, "Behold my beloved Son, hear him." I then addressed this second person, saying, "O Lord, what church shall I join?" He replied, "Don't join any of them; they are all corrupt." The vision then vanished.[41]

That's a good summary of the vision—short and crisp for its intended audience, a journalist. But there was much more to the story.

10 TRIAL

Joseph provided more details in other accounts, details that show what he experienced as a teenager. When he went out to pray, young Joseph was probably both eager and nervous. He had something serious on his mind, and he didn't want his family members or neighbors interrupting or making fun of him. What if his dad stumbled onto him? How would Joseph explain what he was doing to a man who didn't believe in joining churches?

In his 1835 account of the vision, Joseph recounted that after kneeling, "I heard a noise behind me like some person walking towards me. . . . The noise of walking seemed to draw nearer. I sprung up on my feet . . . and looked around but saw no person or thing that was calculated to produce the noise of walking. I kneeled again."[42]

Being interrupted was not the biggest fear Joseph faced. Even more frightening than something he could see was a power he could not see. He faced an invisible opponent that soon gripped him. He explained:

> Having looked around me and finding myself alone, I kneeled down and began to offer up the desires of my heart to God. I had scarcely done so, when immediately I was seized upon by some power which entirely overcame me and had such astonishing influence over me as to bind my tongue so that I could not speak. Thick darkness gathered around me, and it seemed to me for a time as if I were doomed to sudden destruction.

What was this foe? Distress?[43] Anxiety?[44] His imagination?

Joseph quickly realized it was something far worse. He felt himself, he said, about "to sink into despair and abandon myself to destruction, not to an imaginary ruin but to the power of some actual being from the unseen world who had such a marvelous power as I had never before felt in any being."[45]

This was not what he had expected. Back when he encountered the scripture that told him he could get an answer directly from God, he rejoiced. According to Orson Pratt, "This was cheering information to him: tidings that gave him great joy. It was like a light shining forth in a dark place, to guide him to the path in which he should walk."[46]

Yet the force that now seized him was exactly the opposite: vile, evil, seeking to smother his good thoughts with bad. According to Orson Hyde, "The adversary . . . made several strenuous efforts to cool his ardent soul. He filled his mind with doubts and brought to mind all manner of inappropriate images to prevent him from obtaining the object of his endeavors."[47]

Right at the moment when the teenage Joseph was seeking forgiveness for his sins, he instead experienced doubts and a flurry of distracting thoughts. Joseph fought against these thoughts and the evil force that seemed about to smother him. Succeeding in this fight took every ounce of strength Joseph could muster. And by this point in his life, that was a lot.

11 FORGIVENESS

Joseph was no longer the sickly bag of bones his mother easily carried around when he was seven. The Smith men were all big for their time, and at age fourteen, Joseph may already have been approaching his six-foot adult height. Moreover, hard physical labor built his muscles, making him a strong physical specimen.

To succeed in his battle with the adversary, Joseph fought with all his might. He recounted:

Exerting all my powers to call upon God to deliver me out of the power of this enemy which had seized upon me, and at the very moment when I was ready to sink into despair and abandon myself to destruction . . . . Just at this moment of great alarm, I saw a pillar of light exactly over my head above the brightness of the sun, which descended ... gradually until it fell upon me. It no sooner appeared than I found myself delivered from the enemy which held me bound.[48]

Relieved to be free, Joseph now faced what appeared to be an equally disturbing prospect: being burned alive. As a nineteenth-century boy, he had seen only *natural* light in his day, and with odd exceptions like fireflies, that light came from a single source, which was fire. With intense light descending on top of him, the teenager naturally wondered if the fire would consume him. According to Orson Pratt:

> He continued praying, while the light appeared to be gradually descending towards him; and, as it drew nearer, it increased in brightness, and magnitude, so that, by the time that it reached the tops of the trees, the whole wilderness, for some distance around, was illuminated in a most glorious and brilliant manner. He expected to have seen the leaves and boughs of the trees consumed, as soon as the light came in contact with them; but, perceiving that it did not produce that effect, he was encouraged with the hopes of being able to endure its presence. It continued descending, slowly, until it rested upon the

earth, and he was enveloped in the midst of it. When it first came upon him, it produced a peculiar sensation throughout his whole system; and, immediately, his mind was caught away, from the natural objects with which he was surrounded; and he was enwrapped in a heavenly vision.[49]

In Joseph's 1835 account, he explained what happened next:

A pillar of fire appeared above my head, it presently rested down upon my . . . head, and filled me with joy unspeakable. A personage appeared in the midst of this pillar of flame which was spread all around, and yet nothing consumed. Another personage soon appeared like unto the first. He said unto me, "Thy sins are forgiven thee."[50]

12 ANSWERS

The main reason Joseph wanted to know which church to join was that he was burdened with sin and hoped to find forgiveness through a church. The assurance from God that his sins were forgiven fulfilled his deepest wish. The Lord also told him not to join any existing churches, including the Methodist church, the religious group he favored and about which he asked specifically.[51] According to Orson Hyde, "He was further commanded to wait patiently until some future time, when the true doctrine of Christ and the complete truth of the gospel would be revealed to him."[52]

There was much more to the vision than Joseph ever fully recorded. "I saw many angels in this vision," he noted in his 1835 account.[53] In another history, he said of the Lord, "Many other things did he say unto me which I cannot write at this time."[54]

When the vision ended, Joseph had two feelings simultaneously. The first was exquisite joy. Orson Pratt explained, "The vision withdrew, leaving his mind in a state of calmness and peace indescribable."[55] The guilt of sin had lifted. In his handwritten 1832 account, Joseph said, "My soul was filled with love, and for many days I could rejoice with great joy, and the Lord was with me."[56] But along with this joy, there was also the sheer exhaustion that sometimes follows spiritual experiences. According to Alexander Neibaur's account, when the vision ended, Joseph "endeavored to arise but felt uncommon feeble."[57]

13 FACING MOTHER

"When the light had departed," Joseph recalled, "I had no strength, but soon recovering in some degree I went home." Should he tell his parents? the teenage prophet likely wondered. Probably not; at least not yet. Would they even believe him, or would they continue to assert their own religious notions? Yet even if he didn't tell them, he felt really weak, and they might notice.

Sure enough. Moms and dads can often tell when something's up with their children.

"As I leaned up to the fire piece," Joseph wrote rather formally years later, "Mother enquired what the matter was. I replied, 'Never mind. All is well. I am well enough off.'"

That was true. He *was* well off—probably better than ever—from a spiritual standpoint. But, of course, his wise and observant mother could still detect that things weren't normal with him. Joseph had to say something else to satisfy her worry, and he did. "I then told my mother," he recorded, that "I have learned for myself that Presbyterianism is not true."[58] That is about as close to the topic as he seemed to want to get at the time.

14 REJECTION

Not that Joseph didn't want to talk about the vision. He really did. But when teenage boys want to spill their innermost secrets, especially when they worry about being criticized, they are sometimes very careful about picking the person they tell. If Dad might be skeptical and Mom might put pressure on him again to join her church, which he didn't want to do, who could he tell? Who would understand? Joseph decided he would go to a leader of the Methodists, the group he liked the most among the existing churches of the day.

Which Methodist leader did he approach? Was it George Lane? Very likely, though he didn't record the man's name. Here is what Joseph said:

Some few days after I had this vision, I happened to be in company with one of the Methodist preachers who was very active in the before-mentioned religious excitement, and conversing with him on the subject of religion, I took occasion to give him an account of the vision which I had had.

If the leader *was* George Lane, Joseph probably thought that if anyone could understand him, it would be this man, this great preacher whose sermons had encouraged others to get religion, to be converted, to have a personal spiritual experience. And now Joseph had gotten one, just as the minister had preached.

This was not, however, the kind of experience the preacher had expected. Stories of personal conversion and forgiveness were one thing, but something Joseph said set the minister off.[59] Did Joseph repeat what the Lord told him about the churches of the day?

Whatever Joseph said, the preacher clearly felt threatened. "I was greatly surprised at his behavior," Joseph related. "He treated my communication not only lightly but with great contempt, saying it was all of the devil, that there was no such thing as visions or revelations in these days, that all such things had ceased with the apostles and that there never would be any more of them."[60]

Joseph had trusted the preacher with his innermost thoughts, something he didn't tell even his parents, something that made him feel vulnerable. Now, however, instead of receiving understanding from this man he deeply respected, Joseph faced what every teenager hates: rejection.[61]

It would have been bad enough had it been just the preacher. But the minister didn't keep Joseph's communication confidential. Joseph grieved:

> I soon found . . . that my telling the story . . . excited a great deal of prejudice against me among professors of religion and was the cause of great persecution which continued to increase. And though I was an obscure boy only between fourteen and fifteen years of age, and my circumstances in life such as to make a boy of no consequence in the world, yet men of high standing would take notice sufficiently to excite the public mind against me and create a hot persecution. And this was common among all the sects. All united to persecute me.[62]

15 GOING QUIET

How was it, Joseph wondered, that these great men were suddenly paying attention to a poor farm boy? "But strange or not," Joseph said, "so it was, and was often the cause of great sorrow to myself." Joseph now found himself trying to explain his very personal experience to others. He had to in order to defend himself against the criticism. "But," Joseph wrote in his 1832 account, "I could find none that would believe the heavenly vision."[63]

So he did what teenage boys do when people reject them: he clammed up. If people refused to believe him, he'd just stop talking about his vision.[64]

Over the ensuing decade and a half, Joseph told the story privately only to trusted individuals and recorded it in his early personal history. But he hesitated to mention it publicly. For example, his good friend and scribe Oliver Cowdery (to whom he had confided his First Vision experience) began writing a series of letters that were included in *The Latter Day Saints' Messenger and Advocate*—a religious newspaper—as a way of publishing Joseph's early history.

In his third letter, Oliver wrote of Joseph, "I come to the fifteenth year of his life." Oliver recounted "the great awakening, or excitement raised on the subject of religion," and in the process, he mentioned Reverend Lane and how Joseph's "mind became awakened." He went on at some length, but his published letter ended before relating how Joseph went into the woods to pray.[65]

After this letter was published, Joseph must have told Oliver that he didn't want to see the First Vision account in print. Several weeks later, when Oliver took up the pen to write his next letter, he composed the following awkward explanation for his change in plans:

> You will recollect that I mentioned the time of a religious excitement in Palmyra and vicinity to have been in the fifteenth year of our brother J. Smith Jr.'s age. That was an

error in the type—it should have been in the seventeenth.... This would bring the date down to the year 1823. I do not deem it to be necessary to write further on the subject of this excitement.[66]

Despite Joseph's hesitation to bring up the topic in public, one thing he would never do was deny what had happened to him. He simply couldn't. "It was ... a fact," he later wrote, "that I had had a vision," and it bothered him that people wanted him to deny what he had actually seen. "I had seen a vision," he affirmed. "I knew it, and I knew that God knew it, and I could not deny it, neither dare I do it. At least I knew that by so doing I would offend God and come under condemnation."[67]

16 TEMPTATIONS

Yet like most teenagers, he wanted people to like him. He wanted acceptance. And that put all kinds of pressure on him, especially when he wouldn't deny his vision. Some people probably shunned him altogether. Many likely considered him weird or, in any case, not the kind of person to hang around if you wanted others to like you. What made it worse was that God promised to reveal more to him at some future date, and that day didn't come immediately.[68]

When someone promises to get back to a teenager, the teenager often thinks in terms of days or weeks, not months or years. More than three years would pass before Joseph received *any* further communication from God beyond the normal promptings provided by the Light of

Christ. What did that mean to the young prophet? Like many a teenager, Joseph began to doubt himself, to worry about his worthiness. Had he forfeited his sacred calling?

"During the space of time which intervened between the time I had the vision and the year 1823," Joseph said, "having been forbidden to join any of the religious sects of the day, and being of very tender years and persecuted by those who ought to have been my friends and to have treated me kindly, and if they supposed me to be deluded to have endeavored in a proper and affectionate manner to have reclaimed me, I was left to all kinds of temptations. And mingling with all kinds of society, I frequently fell into many foolish errors and displayed the weakness of youth and the corruption of human nature which I am sorry to say led me into divers temptations to the gratification of many appetites offensive in the sight of God."[69]

What exactly did he do? He didn't give specifics, and his clerks later softened the language of the account before publishing it.[70]

But one thing is clear. The young man who felt the indescribable joy of repentance and being forgiven by God now felt burdened by sin again. Doctrine and Covenants 20:5 explains, "After it was truly manifested unto [Joseph] that he had received a remission of his sins, he was entangled again in the vanities of the world." In 1832, Joseph told Frederick G. Williams, "I fell into transgressions and sinned in many things which brought a wound upon my soul, and there were many things which transpired that cannot be written."[71] Later Joseph said, "In consequence of these things I often felt condemned for my weakness and imperfections."[72]

Such feelings were not unusual. Most people feel that way to some degree during their teenage years and beyond.

17 A MESSENGER

Like most human beings, Joseph struggled as a teenager. He struggled with rejection, struggled to find friends, struggled to feel worthy. Then finally, by the evening of September 21, 1823—when he was three months shy of his eighteenth birthday—he was ready to put his life in order again. Orson Hyde wrote that after Joseph "lapsed into the errors and vanities of the world," he was later "genuinely sorry for" them.[73] As Orson Pratt put it, Joseph "sincerely and truly repented."[74] He felt godly remorse and wanted to know once again that he had been forgiven. He wanted to feel the exquisite joy that followed his First Vision.

Teenagers sometimes stay up late at night after other family members have gone to bed and are sound asleep. Joseph, full of worry about his spiritual state, did just that on this occasion. Oliver Cowdery, in his flowery way, left the following account of the circumstances:

On the evening of the 21st of September, 1823, previous to retiring to rest, our brother's mind was unusually wrought up on the subject which had so long agitated his mind. His heart was drawn out in fervent prayer, and his whole soul was so lost to everything of a temporal nature, that earth, to him, had lost its charms, and all he desired was to be prepared in heart to commune with some kind messenger who could communicate to him the desired information of his acceptance with God.

Joseph, lying in the crowded upper loft of the log home next to his brothers, decided to pray as his brothers one by one fell asleep beside him, leaving him in temporary privacy to pour out his heart to God. Oliver's account relates:

In this situation, hours passed unnumbered. How many or how few I know not, neither is he able to inform me, but supposes it must have been eleven or twelve [o'clock], and perhaps later, as the noise and bustle of the family, in retiring, had long since ceased. While continuing in prayer for a manifestation in some way that his sins were forgiven—endeavoring to exercise faith in the scriptures—on a sudden, a light like that of day, only of a purer and far more glorious appearance and brightness, burst into the room. Indeed, to use his own description, the first sight was as though the house was filled with consuming and unquenchable fire. This sudden appearance of a light so bright, as must naturally be expected, occasioned a shock or sensation, visible to the extremities of the body. It was, however, followed with a calmness and serenity of mind, and an overwhelming rapture of joy that surpassed understanding. And in a moment, a personage stood before him.[75]

Having previously experienced a glorious vision, Joseph adjusted to this one rapidly. Briefly startled by the fire-like glory once again, he knew the seeming flames that now engulfed him would not hurt him, and he enjoyed once more the rapturous emotions that filled his soul during his First Vision.[76]

Using scripture-like language, Joseph described this new experience as follows in his 1832 history:

And it came to pass, when I was seventeen years of age, I called again upon the Lord, and he shewed unto me a heavenly vision. For behold, an angel of the Lord came and stood before me. And it was by night. And he called me by name, and he said the Lord had forgiven me my sins. And he revealed unto me that in the town of Manchester, Ontario County, New York, there was plates of gold upon which there was engravings which was engraven by Moroni and his fathers, . . . and that I should go and get them.[77]

18 THE THIRD TIME

Latter-day Saints will recognize the more familiar account of the angel's visit found in Joseph's later history, a portion of which was canonized as Joseph Smith—History in the Pearl of Great Price. In this later history, Joseph detailed the three successive visits of the angel that night, the third of which he described as follows:

But what was my surprise when again I beheld the same messenger at my bedside and heard him rehearse or repeat over again to me the same things as before and added a caution to me, telling me that Satan would try to tempt me (in consequence of the indigent circumstances of my father's family) to get the plates for the purpose of getting rich. This he forbid me, saying that I must have no . . . other object in view in getting the plates but to glorify God and must not be influenced by any other motive but that of building his kingdom. Otherwise, I could not get them. After this third visit, he again ascended up into heaven as before, and I was again left to ponder on the strangeness of what I had just experienced, when almost immediately after the heavenly messenger had ascended from me the third time, the cock crew, and I found that day was approaching so that our interviews must have occupied the whole of that night.[78]

19 TELLING FATHER

This last warning that Joseph received about his motives for getting the gold plates fit the teenager's circumstances well. Joseph's family had to work hard from before sunup to after sundown to eke out an existence on the farm they were trying to purchase. On top of that, they had to make annual payments on the property, which they were buying on contract, and coming up with cash in a largely barter-based economy was tough. The family had also begun building a larger frame home to replace their old log one, and that added financial obligations for material and the labor of a contractor.[79]

The relentless work of the farm weighed heavily on Joseph the morning after the angel's three visits. Besides the exhaustion that often accompanies spiritual experiences, Joseph had to deal with the fact that he hadn't gotten any sleep. Stringing two hard days of farm work together without any rest in between was understandably hard on him.

And the seventeen-year-old bore another burden. During the all-night interview, the angel had told him he needed to talk with his father and tell him everything the angel said. That direction scared Joseph, who hated rejection and wasn't sure his dad would believe him.[80]

It was September 22—early fall—and time to harvest grain the family had sown on a cleared portion of the property. This was a grueling task done by hand in those days. According to Joseph's mother, he was out in the field that morning reaping with his father and elder brother Alvin, "when," she said:

> Joseph stopped quite suddenly; and seemed to be in a very deep study. Alvin, observing this, hurried him, saying, "We must not slacken our hands, or we will not be able to complete our task." Upon which, Joseph went to work again, and after laboring a short time, he stopped just as he had done before. As this was something quite unusual and strange, it attracted the attention of his father; and upon which he

discovered that Joseph was very pale; and supposing that he was sick, told him to go to the house and have his mother doctor him.[81]

Between the old log home, where the Smiths were still living, and the grain field was an apple orchard, surrounded by a fence.[82] Joseph said, "I started with the intention of going to the house, but in attempting to cross the fence out of the field where we were, my strength entirely failed me, and I fell helpless on the ground and for a time was quite unconscious of anything."[83]

"He was here but a short time," his mother explained, "when the messenger, whom he saw the previous night, visited him again. And the first thing he said was, 'Why did you not tell your father what I commanded you to tell him?' Joseph replied, 'I was afraid my father would not believe me.' The angel rejoined, 'he will believe every word you say to him.'"[84]

The angel, Joseph recorded later, "again related unto me all that he had related to me the previous night, and commanded me to go to my father and tell him of the vision and commandments which I had received."[85] It took courage for the teenager to tell his father, but being willing to do whatever the Lord now required of him was proof that he was truly repentant.

"I obeyed," Joseph said simply in his history. "I returned back to my father in the field and rehearsed the whole matter to him."

To young Joseph's immense relief, his work-hardened father wept, replied that what Joseph experienced "was of God," and told him "to go and do as commanded by the messenger."[86]

20 CONCLUSION

Joseph did as he was commanded but continued to struggle at times, making mistakes and repenting of them. It took four years before the Lord was willing to entrust the sacred plates to him. He finally qualified to receive them, but even after that, he made mistakes, and the Lord chastised him for his failings and helped him get back on track.[87] With each struggle, his understanding increased, and he grew a little bit more until he finally fulfilled the mission for which he was foreordained.

Like Joseph Smith Jr., all people struggle. When God the Father first appeared to Joseph, he called him by name. The Savior then addressed him as "Joseph, my son." When Moroni appeared to Joseph three years later, he also called him by name. God knows your name too. He knows everything about you, including what you are supposed to do in life. He feels what you feel and understands what you need. After Joseph's First Vision, the teenager testified, "I have learned for myself."[88]

If you do what Joseph did—seek a testimony of God, repent of your sins, strive to live as you should, and work to receive your own revelation—the Lord will work with you and help you grow to fulfill the mission to which you have been foreordained. And like Joseph, you can experience great joy in your service, even if at times it is disrupted by the strains of mortality.

ABOUT THE AUTHOR

Richard E. Turley Jr. is a former Assistant Church Historian and Recorder of The Church of Jesus Christ of Latter-day Saints. He helped found the Joseph Smith Papers project and served as chair of its editorial board. He has published many books on Latter-day Saint and Western U.S. history and is the recipient of numerous prizes for his historical work and writing, including the American Historical Association's Herbert Feis Award for distinguished contributions to public history.

SOURCES

Sometimes people ask why Joseph Smith didn't write down his early experiences when he had them. In the spring of 1820, for example, why didn't he go home and record the First Vision right after it happened? Why didn't he record the visits of the angel Moroni on September 21 and 22, 1823? Why did he wait until years later?

The answer is simple: because he didn't record anything. He was a poor farm boy with little formal education. Paper was expensive, and writing was not an activity he enjoyed. He didn't seem to understand the value of recording his experiences until he translated the Book of Mormon and read the many passages that talk about the importance of record-keeping. At that point, he began spotty recording of revelations.

Only later after the Church was organized and he received direct commandments to keep records did he begin making efforts to keep a regular history, going back to record his earlier experiences. Yet even then, record-keeping was hard for him given all the other demands on his time and resources. We are fortunate to have what we do from him. Frankly, most members of the Church today are not much different, neglecting to keep personal records of their own spiritual experiences despite repeated direction from leaders to do so.

I personally am grateful for the heroic efforts Joseph made, at times against great odds, to obey the Lord's commandments to keep records. May we do as well as he did and appreciate the precious accounts he left for us.

For the sake of readability, I have modernized the spelling, capitalization, and punctuation in quotations in the text that are taken from the sources below.

[1]Karen Lynn Davidson, David J. Whittaker, Mark Ashurst-McGee, Richard L. Jensen, eds. *Histories, Volume 1: Joseph Smith Histories 1832-1844*, vol. 1 of the Histories series of *The Joseph Smith Papers,* ed. Dean C. Jessee, Ronald

K. Esplin, and Richard Lyman Bushman (Salt Lake City: Church Historian's Press, 2012), 11; http://www.joseph smithpapers.org/paper-summary/history-circa-summer-1832/1.

2 *The Travels of Capts. Lewis and Clarke* (London: Longman, Hurst, Rees, and Orme, 1809), 24.

3 Richard L. Bushman, *Joseph Smith and the Beginnings of Mormonism* (Urbana: University of Illinois Press, 1984), 8.

4 Bushman, *Joseph Smith and the Beginnings*, 11-12.

5 Lavina Fielding Anderson, ed., *Lucy's Book: A Critical Edition of Lucy Mack Smith's Family Memoir* (Salt Lake City: Signature Books, 2001), 312-13.

6 Richard L. Bushman, *Joseph Smith: Rough Stone Rolling* (New York: Alfred A. Knopf, 2005), 19.

7 LeRoy S. Wirthlin, "Joseph Smith's Boyhood Operation: An 1813 Surgical Success," *BYU Studies* 21, no. 2 (1981): 146.

8 http://www.josephsmithpapers.org/paper-summary/ history-1838-1856-volume-a-1-23-december-1805-30-august-1834/137.

9 Wirthlin, "Joseph Smith's Boyhood Operation," 148.

10 Anderson, *Lucy's Book*, 309.

11 Anderson, *Lucy's Book*, 310.

12 Bushman, *Rough Stone Rolling*, 21.

13 Wirthlin, "Joseph Smith's Boyhood Operation," 153.

14 http://www.josephsmithpapers.org/paper-summary /history-1838-1856-volume-a-1-23-december-1805-30-august-1834/137.

15 Bushman, *Rough Stone Rolling*, 21; http://www.joseph smith papers.org/paper-summary/history-1838-1856-volume-d-1-1-august-1842-1-july-1843/277?highlight

=bone.

[16] Bushman, *Rough Stone Rolling,* 28.

[17] http://www.josephsmithpapers.org/paper-summary/history-1838-1856-volume-a-1-23-december-1805-30-august1834/137?highlight =crutches.

[18] James H. Hotchkin, *A History of the Purchase and Settlement of Western New York* (New York: M. W. Dodd, 1848), 130.

[19] Daniel Walker Howe, *What Hath God Wrought: The Transformation of America, 1815-1848* (New York: Oxford University Press, 2007), 497; Michel Chevalier, *Society, Manners, and Politics in the United States,* trans. T. Bradford (Boston, 1839), 317.

[20] History, Circa Summer 1832, in *JSP,* H1:11; http://www.josephsmithpapers.org/paper-summary/history-circa-summer-1832/1.

[21] Anderson, *Lucy's Book,* 344.

[22] History, Circa Summer 1832, in *JSP,* H1:11-12; http://www.josephsmithpapers.org/paper-summary/history-circa-summer-1832/1.

[23] History, Circa Summer 1832, in *JSP,* H1:12; http://www.josephsmithpapers.org/paper-summary/history-circa-summer-1832/2.

[24] Bushman, *Rough Stone Rolling,* 33.

[25] Donald L. Enders, "The Sacred Grove," *Ensign* 20 (Apr. 1990): 14.

[26] Donald L. Enders, "A Snug Log House," *Ensign* 15 (Aug. 1985): 16.

[27] History, Circa Summer 1832, in *JSP,* H1:12; http://www.josephsmithpapers.org/paper-summary/history-circa-summer-1832/2.

28 http://www.josephsmithpapers.org/paper-summary/history-1838-1856-volume-a-1-23-december-1805-30-august-1834/2; Joseph Smith—History 1:5-7.

29 Bushman, *Joseph Smith and the Beginnings*, 36.

30 Bushman, *Rough Stone Rolling*, 37.

31 Bushman, *Joseph Smith and the Beginnings*, 54.

32 http://www.josephsmithpapers.org/paper-summary/alexander-neibaur-journal-24-may-1844-extract/1.

33 "Letter III [Oliver Cowdery to W. W. Phelps]," *Latter Day Saints' Messenger and Advocate* 1, no. 3 (Dec. 1834): 42.

34 *The Life and Times of Rev. George Peck, D.D.* (New York: Nelson & Phillips; Cincinnati: Hitchcock & Walden, 1874), 108-9. For an even earlier account of this same meeting, see George Peck, *Early Methodism Within the Bounds of the Old Genesee Conference from 1788 to 1828* (New York: Carlton and Porter, 1860), 314-15.

35 J. W. Peterson, "Another Testimony: Statement of William Smith, Concerning Joseph, the Prophet," *Deseret Evening News*, Jan. 20, 1894, p. 11.

36 http://www.josephsmithpapers.org/paper-summary/history-circa-june-1839-circa-1841-draft-2/2; Joseph Smith—History 1:12.

37 http://www.josephsmithpapers.org/paper-summary/history-circa-june-1839-circa-1841-draft-2/3; Joseph Smith—History 1:13.

38 Enders, "Snug Log House," 16-17.

39 https://www.josephsmithpapers.org/paper-summary/history-1838-1856-volume-a-1-23-december-1805-30-august-1834/3; Joseph Smith—History 1:14.

40 http://www.josephsmithpapers.org/paper-summary/history-circa-june-1839-circa-1841-draft-2/3; Joseph

Smith—History 1:15.

41 http://www.josephsmithpapers.org/paper-summary /interview-21-august-1843-extract/1.

42 Dean C. Jessee, Mark Ashurst-McGee, Richard L. Jensen, eds., *Journals, Volume 1: 1832-1839*, vol. 1 of the Journals series of *The Joseph Smith Papers,* ed. Dean C. Jessee, Ronald K. Esplin, and Richard Lyman Bushman (Salt Lake City: Church Historian's Press, 2008), 88; http://www.josephsmithpapers.org/paper-summary/ journal-1835-1836/25.

43 In the course of his ponderings, Joseph said, "My mind become excedingly distressed." History, Circa Summer 1832, in *JSP*, H1:11; http://www. josephsmith papers.org/paper-summary/history-circa-summer-1832/1.

44 "It was the first time in my life that I had made such an attempt, for amidst all my anxieties I had never as yet made the attempt to pray vocally." http://www.joseph smithpapers.org/paper-summary/history-circa-june-1839- circa-1841-draft-2/3; Joseph Smith—History 1:14.

45 http://www.josephsmithpapers.org/paper- summary/history-circa-june-1839-circa-1841-draft-2/3; Joseph Smith—History 1:16.

46 http://www.josephsmithpapers.org/paper-summary /appendix-orson-pratt-an-interesting-account-of-several- remarkable-visions-1840/4.

47 http://www.josephsmithpapers.org/paper-summary /orson-hyde-ein-ruf-aus-der-wste-a-cry-out-of-the- wilderness-1842-extract-english-translation/1.

48 http://www.josephsmithpapers.org/paper-summary /history-circa-june-1839-circa-1841-draft-2/3; Joseph Smith—History 1:16-17.

[49] http://www.josephsmithpapers.org/paper-summary /appendix-orson-pratt-an-interesting-account-of-several-remarkable-visions-1840/5.

[50] http://www.josephsmithpapers.org/paper-summary /journal-1835-1836/25.

[51] Dean C. Jessee, ed., *The Papers of Joseph Smith* (Salt Lake City: Deseret Book, 1989), 1:461; http://www. josephsmithpapers.org/paper-summary/alexander-neibaur-journal-24-may-1844-extract/1.

[52] Jessee, *Papers of Joseph Smith*, 1:409; http://www. josephsmithpapers.org/paper-summary/orson-hyde-ein-ruf-aus-der-wste-a-cry-out-of-the-wilderness-1842-extract-english-translation/1.

[53] Journal, 1835-1836, in *JSP*, J1:88; http://www.joseph smithpapers.org/paper-summary/journal-1835-1836/25.

[54] http://www.josephsmithpapers.org/paper-summary /history-circa-june-1839-circa-1841-draft-2/3; Joseph Smith—History 1:20.

[55]History, Circa Summer 1832, in *JSP*, H1:523-24; http://www.josephsmithpapers.org/paper-summary/ appendix-orson-pratt-an-interesting-account-of-several-remarkable-visions-1840/5.

[56] History, Circa Summer 1832, in *JSP*, H1:13; http:// www.josephsmithpapers.org/paper-summary/history-circa-summer-1832/3.

[57] Jessee, *Papers of Joseph Smith*, 1:461; http://www. joseph smithpapers.org/paper-summary/alexander-neibaur-journal-24-may-1844-extract/2.

[58] http://www.josephsmithpapers.org/paper-summary /history-1838-1856-volume-a-1-23-december-1805-30-august-1834/138; Joseph Smith—History 1:20.

[59] Bushman, *Rough Stone Rolling,* 41; Steven C. Harper, *First Vision: Memory and Mormon Origins* (New York: Oxford University Press, 2019), 12n7.

[60] http://www.josephsmithpapers.org/paper-summary /history-circa-june-1839-circa-1841-draft-2/3; Joseph Smith—History 1:21.

[61] Harper, *First Vision,* 9-12.

[62] http://www.josephsmithpapers.org/paper-summary /history-circa-june-1839-circa-1841-draft-2/4; Joseph Smith—History 1:22.

[63] History, Circa Summer 1832, in *JSP,* H1:13; http:// www.josephsmithpapers.org/paper-summary/history-circa-summer-1832/3.

[64] Harper, *First Vision,* 11.

[65] Cowdery, "Letter III," 43.

[66] Oliver Cowdery, "Letter IV," *Latter Day Saints' Messenger and Advocate* 1 (Feb. 1835): 77-78.

[67] http://www.josephsmithpapers.org/paper-summary /history-circa-june-1839-circa-1841-draft-2/4; Joseph Smith—History 1:25.

[68] Jessee, *Papers of Joseph Smith,* 1:409; http://www. josephsmithpapers.org/paper-summary/orson-hyde-ein-ruf-aus-der-wste-a-cry-out-of-the-wilderness-1842-extract-english-translation/1.

[69] http://www.josephsmithpapers.org/paper-summary /history-circa-june-1839-circa-1841-draft-2/5; Joseph Smith—History 1:28.

[70] http://www.josephsmithpapers.org/paper-summary /history-1838-1856-volume-a-1-23-december-1805-30-august-1834/139.

[71] History, Circa Summer 1832, in *JSP,* H1:13;

http://www.josephsmithpapers.org/paper-summary/history-circa-summer-1832/4.

[72] http://www.josephsmithpapers.org/paper-summary/history-circa-june-1839-circa-1841-draft-2/5; Joseph Smith—History 1:27.

[73] Jessee, *Papers of Joseph Smith*, 1:409; http://www.josephsmithpapers.org/paper-summary/orson-hyde-ein-ruf-aus-der-wste-a-cry-out-of-the-wilderness-1842-extract-english-translation/1.

[74] History, Circa Summer 1832, in *JSP*, H1:524; http://www.josephsmithpapers.org/paper-summary/appendix-orson-pratt-an-interesting-account-of-several-remarkable-visions-1840/6.

[75] Cowdery, "Letter IV," 78-79.

[76] "His whole person was glorious beyond description, and his countenance truly like lightning. The room was exceedingly light, but not so very bright as immediately around his person. When I first looked upon him I was afraid, but the fear soon left me." http://www.josephsmithpapers.org/paper-summary/history-1838-1856-volume-a-1-23-december-1805-30-august-1834/5.

[77] History, Circa Summer 1832, in *JSP*, H1:4; http://www.josephsmithpapers.org/paper-summary/history-circa-summer-1832/4.

[78] http://www.josephsmithpapers.org/paper-summary/history-1838-1856-volume-a-1-23-december-1805-30-august-1834/6; Joseph Smith—History 1:47.

[79] Anderson, *Lucy's Book*, 349; Bushman, *Rough Stone Rolling*, 47; Enders, "Snug Log House," 19.

[80] Anderson, *Lucy's Book*, 340.

[81] Anderson, *Lucy's Book*, 339.

[82] Anderson, *Lucy's Book,* 340.

[83] http://www.josephsmithpapers.org/paper-summary /history-1838-1856-volume-a-1-23-december-1805-30- august-1834/7; Joseph Smith—History 1:48.

[84] Anderson, *Lucy's Book,* 340.

[85] http://www.josephsmithpapers.org/paper-summary /history-1838-1856-volume-a-1-23-december-1805-30- august-1834/7; Joseph Smith—History 1:49.

[86] http://www.josephsmithpapers.org/paper-summary /journal-1835-1836/26; http://www.josephsmithpapers .org/paper-summary/history-1838-1856-volume-a-1-23- december-1805-30-august-1834/7; Joseph Smith—History 1:49.

[87] See, e.g., Doctrine and Covenants 3:6-10; 10:1-3; 21:8, 35:18-19; 64:5-7; 132:50, 60.

[88] Joseph Smith—History 1:20.

Made in the USA
San Bernardino, CA
02 April 2020